# 100

## THINGS TO DO IN
## NASHVILLE
## BEFORE YOU
# DIE

• • • • • • • • • • • • • • • • • • • • •

# ABBY WHITE

REEDY PRESS

St. Louis, Missouri

To Jackson and Piper,
in the hopes that they will
visit me in Nashville.

Reedy Press
PO Box 5131
St. Louis, MO 63139, USA
www.reedypress.com

Library of Congress Control Number:

ISBN: 978-1-935806-70-7

Design by Jill Halpin

Printed in the United States of America
14 15 16 17 18    5 4 3 2 1

Please note that websites, phone numbers, addresses, and company names are subject to change or cancellation. We did our best to relay the most accurate information available, but due to circumstances beyond our control, please do not hold us liable for misinformation. When exploring new destinations, please do your homework before you go.

For more information, upcoming author events, and book signings, please visit us on Facebook at 100ThingsNashville.

# CONTENTS

**Culture & History**

# PREFACE

Before you turn another page, I want to be completely honest with you: I am not a native Nashvillian.

Wait! Don't put the book down. Let me explain why you should keep reading it, whether you were born and raised in the 615 or if you traveled all the way from Poughkeepsie for a quick visit. I love this city. I've loved it since the moment I moved here, sight unseen, 13 years ago. I was amazed at the way in which a community could embrace a clueless recent college graduate who was just trying to figure out what to do with her life. I learned very quickly that doing good, hard work will take you far in this little big town, whether you work on Music Row or at Vanderbilt University Medical Center.

As a journalist, I've been fortunate to partake in quintessential Nashville experiences and things that would definitely fall into the off-the-beaten-path category. I've stood enraptured backstage at The Ryman and embarrassed myself by singing karaoke (badly) at Santa's Pub. I ate the extra hot at Prince's Hot Chicken and lived to tell about it, and I once had four different Bobbie's Dairy Dip shakes in one sitting.

It's been incredible watching the rest of the world's reaction to the booming growth of our beloved city. They've hailed us as everything from "It City" (thanks, *New York Times*) to one of the five best places to visit in the whole world (gracias, *Conde Nast Traveler*). It's been so much fun to watch everyone fall in love with Nashville, and I'm assuming you have a little love affair with it too, or you wouldn't be holding this book right now.

But even if you're a Nashville native, I bet there are things you haven't done here, things that would top most tourists' lists, like touring the Country Music Hall of Fame or even catching a show at the Grand Ole Opry. Perhaps we could all use a reminder about all of the incredible things this city has to offer, and a primer on some unturned stones and unexplored corners? I mean, when the city you live in is as awesome as Nashville, it's not so ridiculous to be a homegrown tourist, is it?

So, as a starting point, I offer you 100 things to do. It is my hope that perusing this little book will enrich your relationship with this lovely city, whether you're in it for the long haul or just looking for something casual. In Nashville, we have everything you're looking for, and for a song.

Abby White
October 2013

# 100

## THINGS TO DO IN
## NASHVILLE
## BEFORE YOU
# DIE

# FOOD & DRINK

# TURN UP THE HEAT
## AT PRINCE'S HOT CHICKEN SHACK

You may have heard that some like it hot, but in Nashville, we really like it hot. Our chicken, that is. And the godfather of hot chicken is none other than Thornton Prince, who allegedly was served the cayenne pepper-coated dish by a jealous ladyfriend back in the '30s. His great-niece, Andre Prince Jeffries, is the current proprietor of Prince's Hot Chicken, which the James Beard Foundation honored with their America's Classics Award in 2013. Jeffries brines the bird, then flours, fries, and slathers it in a secret mix of hot spices, serving it on white bread with a stack of dill pickle chips. Newbies may want to start with the mild—which is still pretty hot—but if you think you can handle it, go for the extra hot. But have a cold glass of water ready—you'll need it.

123 Ewing Dr. #3
615-226-9442

CLASSIC, FOODIE, EAST NASHVILLE

Tip:
Want to try them all at once? Visit Nashville on July Fourth and hit the Music City Hot Chicken Festival.

Hot chicken has earned a reputation as the unofficial food of Music City, so the true chicken connoisseur should check out the other high-temperature offerings:

## BOLTON'S SPICY CHICKEN & FISH

Also located on the east side, Bolton's offers spicy chicken and fish, and a kitschy, no-fuss ambiance (you knock on the door to place your order).

624 Main St., 615-254-8015

## HATTIE B'S HOT CHICKEN

This midtown option has no-heat versions for the heatphobic, and their spiciest offering, the Fire Starter, isn't quite as lethal as Prince's extra hot. Unlike at the other outposts, you can order a beer here.

112 19th Ave. S., 615-678-4794, www.hattieb.com

## 400 DEGREES

Sandwiched between SoBro and Rutledge Hill, 400 Degrees is convenient if you're staying downtown, and you can choose the heat level, from zero to 400 for the truly bold.

319 Peabody St., 615-244-4467, www.400degreeshotchicken.com

## PEPPERFIRE HOT CHICKEN

This eastside grab-and-go hotspot is famous for their hot chicken tenders and their deep-fried grilled cheese sandwich.

2821 Gallatin Pk., 615-582-4824, www.pepperfirechicken.com

# GET YOUR
## MEAT & THREE FIX
## AT ARNOLD'S COUNTRY KITCHEN

Located a stone's throw away from the Gulch, this James Beard-winning, no-frills joint is only open for lunch on weekdays, and often has a line extending out the door, so get there early. At this family-run restaurant, meat options rotate daily, as do the sides, with the exception of their famous green beans, turnip greens, mac & cheese, and mashed potatoes. The roast beef is to die for, and if you really want to make it a cheat day, splurge and get the chess pie.

605 8th Ave. S.
615-256-4455

FOODIE, KID FRIENDLY

# DRINK TEA, DO GOOD
## AT THISTLE STOP CAFÉ

The Thistle Stop Café, located off Charlotte in West Nashville, is an extension of social enterprise Thistle Farms, employing graduates of nonprofit Magdalene House, which rehabilitates women who have survived prostitution, trafficking, or addiction, and live on the streets. This beautiful, cozy café serves up healthy breakfast and lunch options, full tea service, and delicious coffee drinks. On Thursdays, they offer intimate live performances in the all-ages, alcohol-free venue. While you're there, be sure to check out Thistle Farms' exceptional body care and home products—you'll definitely want some for yourself.

5128 Charlotte Ave.
615-953-6440
www.thistlestopcafe.org

FOODIE, KID FRIENDLY, SHOPPING

# HOLD NOTHING BACK
## AND GO HOG WILD
## AT MARTIN'S BAR-B-QUE JOINT

People have very strong opinions about barbecue. Pork or beef? Barbeque, BBQ, or bar-b-cue? Naked or sauce? Really, instead of fighting it out, just head to one of Pat Martin's eponymous outposts, where you can choose from pulled pork, smoked chicken, beef brisket, smoked sausage, and smoked turkey sandwiches, tacos, or plates. The classic Martin option is the pulled pork sandwich—cooked whole-hog style over coals and hickory wood for 24 hours—with the Sweet Dixie sauce served with slaw. Some pig, indeed!

7238 Nolensville Rd., Nolensville, 615-776-1856
200 Crossings Lane, Ste. 500, Mt. Juliet, 615-686-2066
Belmont Blvd., Nashville (NOT OPEN YET)
www.martinsbbqjoint.com

FOODIE, KID FRIENDLY

# STAVE OFF A HANGOVER
## AT THE HERMITAGE CAFÉ

The Hermitage Café, a short cab ride from the main drag of downtown Nashville, is open every day from 10 P.M. to 1:30 P.M., so that should tell you a little about the clientele. Let's just say that nobody is going to raise an eyebrow if you stumble in after a long night of rabble-rousing, although house rules dictate that you can't come in unless you can walk in. So, if you can pull yourself together enough to make it to the counter or one of the booths, you'll be rewarded with some of the best greasy-spoon diner food in Nashville. From what we can remember, anyway.

71 Hermitage Ave.
615-254-8871

FOODIE, CLASSIC

# HAVE YOUR CAKE
## AND EAT IT AT FIDO

There are plenty of things to rave about at Hillsboro Village favorite Fido, a hit with power brunchers and college students alike. The local burger is fantastic; the breakfast, lunch, and dinner options varied and inventive; and their coffee is superior. But a true gem lies in the dessert case—if it's available, you can't miss it, due to its electric pink hue. The beet-infused Pink Radio Cake is actually quite sweet and flavorful, and even those who claim to dislike beets will gobble up every morsel. Suitable for a late-night snack or breakfast, because there's vegetables in there!

1812 21st Ave. S.
615-777-3436
www.bongojava.com

FOODIE. KID FRIENDLY

# HAVE A PUPUSA
## AT LAS AMERICAS TAQUERIA

Nashville is a veritable melting pot of different cultures. Nolensville Road is home to a plethora of authentic, internationally inspired restaurants, and one of the best is Salvadorean outpost Las Americas. You might think you're in the wrong spot, as you have to enter through a small market, but in the back of the building is a tiny dining area serving up the best deal in town. The massive pupusas, which cost around two bucks, are crispy and flavorful cornmeal-wrapped discs stuffed with your choice of pork or beans and cheese.

4715 Nolensville Pk.
615-315-8888

FOODIE

# CELEBRATE A SPECIAL
## OCCASION AT THE CATBIRD SEAT
## AT TYPHOON

Since it opened in 2011, The Catbird Seat has remained one of the most desired dining destinations in Nashville for locals and visitors alike. With only 32 seats, the ever-evolving, extraordinary multicourse tasting menu has received rave reviews from the likes of *Bon Appetit, The New York Times,* and *Food & Wine,* to name but a few. The menu is entirely determined by the chefs, with dietary restrictions (provided in advance) taken into consideration. Reservations are necessary for this splurge of a dining experience, so definitely plan ahead if you want to get in and be the envy of your foodie friends.

1711 Division St.
615-810-8200
www.thecatbirdseatrestaurant.com

FOODIE, DATE NIGHT

# AND IF YOU CAN'T GET
## INTO CATBIRD SEAT, HAVE A COCKTAIL
## AT THE PATTERSON HOUSE

If you forgot to make reservations for your night out—or if you just want a really good cocktail—hit The Patterson House, located just below The Catbird Seat. The dark atmosphere has an intimate, pre-Prohibition vibe, and house rules at the joint—no standing or lingering around the bar, no name-dropping—ensure a classy yet relaxed ambiance. The menu is exceptional, and you'll be needing a few of their deviled eggs or tater tots with dill crème fraiche if you have more than one of these potent, expertly crafted beverages. Feeling adventurous? Tell the bartender what you like, and he'll whip up a surprise for you.

1711 Division St.
615-636-7724
www.thepattersonnashville.com

DATE NIGHT, ADULT BEVERAGES

# CELEBRATE SUNDAY FUNDAY
## WITH TWOFERS AT 3 CROW BAR

Sunday Funday is practically a holiday in Nashville, with bars across the city offering two-for-ones for revelers who just aren't quite ready to kiss the weekend goodbye. 3 Crow Bar, located in the epicenter of East Nashville's Five Points, has twofers from noon until "late" for drafts and well drinks. So, you could start the day with a Bloody Mary or four on their back patio, have some PBR-battered chicken tenders for lunch, and watch the sun set with a couple Bushwackers, a popular, delightful, alcohol-infused frozen drink that goes down way too easy.

1024 Woodland St.
615-262-3345
www.3crowbar.com

ADULT BEVERAGES

# FILL YOUR FRIDGE
## WITH LOCAL FARE
## AT THE NASHVILLE FARMERS' MARKET

This daily farmers' market, located just north of downtown in Bicentennial State Park Mall, offers fresh produce, meat, baked goods, and more from area farms and an indoor Market House filled with restaurants and an international market. The interior also hosts the Grow Local Kitchen, offering interactive cooking classes among the many events held at the market. Every weekend, the market hosts a flea market, offering a variety of crafts, clothing, accessories, and home goods year-round.

900 Rosa L Parks Blvd.
615-880-2001
www.nashvillefarmersmarket.org

KID FRIENDLY, FOODIE

# CHEAT ON YOUR DIET
## AT LOVELESS CAFÉ

It's a bit of a hike to get to the famous Loveless Café, but it's worth every single minute of the pretty drive. Whether you're going for breakfast—which you can and should order all day— lunch, or dinner, your best bet is to order one of the family style options for parties of four or more. That way, you can sample as much of this celebrated Southern fare—country ham, hash brown casserole, fried chicken, fried catfish—as possible. Regardless of what you order, do not leave the Loveless without trying their famous biscuits with their homemade peach preserves.

8400 Hwy. 100
615-646-9700
www.lovelesscafe.com

FOODIE, KID FRIENDLY, SCENIC ROUTE

# EAT MORE BACON
## AT THE FARMHOUSE RESTAURANT

We love our bacon in the South, so when somebody finds something new to do with it, we all have to try it and give it our unfiltered opinions. When the Farmhouse opened in SoBro's Encore building in fall 2013, everybody was talking about the cornmeal-encrusted bacon. This versatile, decadent, crispy snack can be enjoyed in a variety of ways; chef Trey Cioccia serves it in jars accompanied by a tiny skillet of preserves, or offers it as a dipping device with a bowl of boiled-peanut hummus. Everything else on the menu is stellar in this cozy yet upscale new hotspot.

210 Almond St.
615-522-0688
www.thefarmhousetn.com

FOODIE

# BEAT THE HEAT
# WITH A SHAKE
## AT BOBBIE'S DAIRY DIP

The tiny ice cream shack in West Nashville has been a summertime staple for Nashvillians for decades. While you certainly can't go wrong with anything you order here, from the delicious dipped cones to the classic sundaes, throw caution and calories to the wind and indulge in one of Bobbie's decadent shakes. Try the Memphis Mafia, a truly deadly combo of vanilla ice cream, malt, peanut butter, banana, and bits of bacon. If you're not down with drinking your bacon, the popular Chubby Checker—twist ice cream, peanut butter, and hot fudge—will have you scraping out your cup with your straw.

5301 Charlotte Ave.
615-463-8088

FOODIE, KID FRIENDLY, CLASSIC

# Tip:

While the sweet treats take center stage at Bobbie's, they also serve up great burgers and some of the best sweet potato fries—accompanied by a slightly sweet-sour cream concoction—you've ever had. Add a shake to that and you've got the perfect mix of salty and sweet.

Also, the original location of Bobbie's is off Charlotte in West Nashville, but Bobbie's has a second outpost at 223 4th Ave. N. in the heart of downtown Nashville.

# LEARN ABOUT
## THE LOCAL BREW
## AT YAZOO BREWING COMPANY

We like to buy local in Nashville, especially our beer, and Yazoo—who celebrated their tenth anniversary in 2013—is beloved by brew aficionados near and far. Take a brewery tour and learn the story behind this tight-knit family business, or take your beer loving to the next level with one of their many "Barely a 5K" runs in which participants don capes and run around, or whiz through the city streets in Big Wheels. Try a flight of beer in the taproom or sample the popular, ever-evolving Hop Project.

910 Division St.
615-891-4649
www.yazoobrew.com

ADULT BEVERAGES

# GET A BURGER
## AT TWIN KEGS

Sometimes the best places to get a good ol' burger are the no-frills ones . . . and Twin Kegs is certainly no-frills. In fact, it's a dive bar: dark, cramped, and smoky. There are sports on the TVs, shuffleboard, karaoke, cheap—but good—beer, and cheap—but really great—bar food. Get the huge "BBB," the Big Bad Burger, which is stacked with bacon and cheese, and you'll be an instant convert. Oh, and if anyone in your party is watching his or her waistline, the menu has healthy options too, but we say go all-out . . . you're at Twin Kegs, after all!

413 W. Thompson Ln.
615-832-3167

FOODIE, ADULT BEVERAGES

# TAKE A SPIN AROUND DOWNTOWN
## ON THE NASHVILLE PEDAL TAVERN

When we heard there was a way to see the city while burning calories while enjoying adult beverages, we had to try out the Nashville Pedal Tavern. The Tavern seats up to 16 revelers and runs up and down the main drags of downtown or midtown Nashville, stopping at various bars and local landmarks. You really do have to pedal to power the Tavern, although your trusty tour guide is the one doing the steering, so nobody is in danger of getting a B.U.I. Reservations are required, and may we recommend wearing sensible footwear?

615-390-5038
www.nashvillepedaltavern.com

ADULT BEVERAGES, GREAT OUTDOORS

# INDULGE YOUR INNER ANGLOPHILE
## AT FLEET STREET PUB

Printer's Alley, located between Third and Fourth avenues in downtown Nashville, is just a stone's throw from the main touristy drag of Lower Broad. Formerly a publishing epicenter and Prohibition playground, it's now filled with nightclubs and karaoke joints, and home to one of the best subterranean watering holes in the city, the English pub-inspired Fleet Street. In addition to some of the finest pub food—fish and chips, shepherd's pie, bangers and mash—in town, the smoker-friendly bar offers an impressive selection of draught beer. Escape for an evening of playing darts, watching football (that's soccer, Americans), and feeding the jukebox before ascending the stairs back up to the real world.

207 Printer's Alley
615-200-0782
www.fleetstreetpub.com

ADULT BEVERAGES, FOODIE

# TAKE A WINE BREAK
## AT RUMOURS IN THE GULCH

The rapidly growing Gulch area of downtown Nashville has welcomed a string of high-rise condo buildings, chain restaurants, and stores in the past decade, but there's still some local heart in this urban playground. The elegant yet casual Rumours, which relocated from its original 12South location in 2013, has a vast, incredible wine list and a friendly, informed staff. The full bar offers mixed drinks and local brews on draught and a fantastic menu. The rotating cheese plate and bruschetta options never disappoint, and Rumours' delicious fried Brussels sprouts—yeah, you read that right—will erase any childhood memories of hiding icky vegetables under the table.

1104 Division St.
615-432-2740
www.rumourswinebar.com

FOODIE, ADULT BEVERAGES

# HAVE A CLASSY DATE
## AT THE OAK BAR

The historic Hermitage Hotel offers some of the most luxurious rooms in the city, but you don't have to book a room to enjoy the hotel's beautifully restored Oak Bar. Located next door to the Capitol Grille—which is great for a nice dinner—the Oak Bar offers an extensive wine list, classic cocktails, and small plates, and a fantastic happy hour from 4:30 to 6:30 P.M. every day. The atmosphere is upscale yet relaxed, and you just might spot a politico or two from nearby Capitol Hill. Just don't fight over politics, or the fried pickles.

231 6th Ave. N.
615-345-7116
www.capitolgrillenashville.com

FOODIE, HISTORIC, ADULT BEVERAGES

# Tip:

If you dine at the Capitol Grille or the Oak Bar, you simply must make a stop in the men's restroom—ladies, that includes you, too. While you'd expect a five-star hotel like The Hermitage to have a pretty nice loo, this Art Deco restroom was named "America's Best Restroom" by Cintas Corporation in 2008. So, go ahead and take that bathroom selfie—it's allowed in this case.

# HAVE AN EAST NASHVILLE GAME DAY
## AT THE VILLAGE PUB AT RIVERSIDE VILLAGE

Sure, there are always plenty of sporting events to watch on TV, but wouldn't you rather play a real game in a bar? Riverside Village's Village Pub—which is Nashville Predators HQ on the East Side for you hockey fans—has a shelf full of fun board games, from Jenga to Taboo. A crowd favorite is the hilarious, slightly evil Cards Against Humanity—like a grown-up Apples to Apples—which will teach you more about your drinking buddies than you may want to know. Order up the Pub's signature mule drink (ginger beer and your pick of poison) and their incredible giant pretzels served with warm Yazoo cheese dip, and you've got a perfect afternoon.

1308 McGavock Pk.
615-942-5880
www.riversidevillagepub.com

FOODIE, ADULT BEVERAGES, EAST NASHVILLE

# CELEBRATE THE FOOD
## THAT'S A UNITER, NOT A DIVIDER
## AT THE TOMATO ART FESTIVAL

One of Nashville's most popular yearly neighborhood events is East Nashville's Tomato Art Festival, held in August in the Five Points area. With a variety of activities that involve a good bit of creativity, humor, and—in some cases—absurdity, this outdoor street fest is free and open to all ages and species (East Nashville is famously dog-friendly). The schedule varies a bit each year, but there's always contests—the Bloody Mary one is always fun—fashion shows, art shows, a 5K, and tons of live music.

Five Points at Woodland and 11th Ave.
www.tomatoartfest.com

GREAT OUTDOORS, KID FRIENDLY
FOODIE, ADULT BEVERAGES

# HAVE BREAKFAST WITH SANTA
## AT THE AQUARIUM RESTAURANT

If you're a kid, what's better than having a meal surrounded by a 200,000-gallon tank filled with 100 different species of tropical fish? Having a meal with Santa while surrounded by a 200,000-gallon tank filled with 100 different species of tropical fish. Opryland's Aquarium Restaurant hosts a breakfast with Santa each year, offering patrons photos with Mr. Claus before or after enjoying a breakfast buffet. Rumor has it that Santa might swim with the fish . . .

KID FRIENDLY

# Did You Know?

After the massive flood engulfed Opryland and much of Nashville in May 2010, one of the wildest stories that circulated was that piranhas had escaped from the Aquarium Restaurant and were swimming around Opry Mills Mall. Several news outlets reported the story, which the restaurant denied. Although the jury is still out regarding the authenticity of the tale, we like to think they're still encircling the food court.

# BE A KID AGAIN,
## BUT WITH ADULT BEVERAGES, AT THE NASHVILLE ZOO

Sure, it's fun to take your kids to the zoo, which you can certainly do here in Nashville, but what's great about our zoo is the fun adult activities—many of which double as fundraisers—that they offer throughout the year. In addition to race courses that take you through the zoo and auctions featuring art created by the zoo animals, one of the most popular events is the yearly Brew at the Zoo. This party features more than 100 craft beers on tap, offerings from food trucks, and evening access to several of the zoo exhibits. When else can you have a beer with a flamingo?

3777 Nolensville Pk.
615-833-1534
www.nashvillezoo.org

KID FRIENDLY, ADULT BEVERAGES
GREAT OUTDOORS, CLASSIC

# Tip:

While we think you'll enjoy going to parties at the zoo, it's of course a wonderful place to take the family. The grounds are well-kept and pretty, and the exhibit areas are large, giving the animals plenty of room to roam. Also, there's a massive, 66,000-square-foot playground, a train, and a carousel, so you can count on having a car filled with exhausted kids on the ride home.

# GO VISIT JACK DANIEL'S
## AT THE JACK DANIEL'S DISTILLERY

You may think it odd that one of the most famous distilleries in the country lies in a dry county, but that's just one of the incredibly weird things about our state. Whiskey aficionados must make the pilgrimage to the home of Jack Daniel's, which is a pretty, one-and-a-half hour drive from Nashville. The distillery offers a free tour, but spring for the extended tour—it's only 10 bucks—and you get an extensive tour and a tasting. Either way, you'll learn a lot about whiskey, prohibition, and Jack himself. Treat yourself or a whiskey-lovin' friend with a personally engraved bottle from the gift shop.

280 Lynchburg Hwy, Lynchburg
931-759-4221
www.jackdaniels.com

ADULT BEVERAGES, SCENIC, HISTORIC

# BUY A DOZEN
## AT THE CUPCAKE COLLECTION

There are many places to buy delicious desserts in Nashville, but The Cupcake Collection offers the sweetest treats of all. The family-run business, overseen by the delightful Mignon Francois, is located in the cutest bright purple house in the heart of Germantown, and they also take their cakes on the road in an old school bus. Mignon and her cupcakes have won several awards since they opened in 2008, including Nashville Scene's Sugar Rush competition and the Best of Nashville reader's poll. You certainly can't go wrong with any of the incredible flavor options, but we recommend the sweet potato, smothered in cream cheese frosting. Yum.

1213 6th Ave N.
615-244-2900
www.thecupcakecollection.com

FOODIE, KID FRIENDLY, CLASSIC

# OTHER RECOMMENDED DESSERT DIET BOMBS

While all of their donuts are superior to anything you'll find at chains, the massive apple fritter from Green Hills mainstay Fox's Donut Den is king. Seriously, it's one of the best things you will ever put in your mouth, especially if you heat it up first. Oh, and Donut Den is open until midnight every night, tempting you into the wee hours.

3900 Hillsboro Pk. Ste. 2, 615-385-1021, www.foxsdonutden.com

Cakes by Leland Riggins of Dessert Designs are a familiar sight at weddings and other events around the city, but the best thing coming out of her kitchen is the sour cream caramel bundt cake. The mix of the dense, flavorful cake and the slightly salty caramel frosting—which the aforementioned cake is absolutely drenched in—will tantalize your taste buds. Order ahead of time online or by calling the bakery, as these cakes are some of the hottest in the city.

850 Hillwood Blvd. Ste. 1, 615-354-9555, dessertdesignsbyleland.com

Jeni's Splendid Ice Creams is based out of Ohio, but we have two outposts here in Nashville; one on the East Side, and one in 12South. In the summertime, expect to see lines out the door, but Jeni's inventive ice cream concoctions are totally worth it. The flavors rotate with the seasons, but if you get a chance, try one of the Nashville-inspired flavors, like Loveless Biscuit + Peach Jam or Yazoo Sue with Rosemary Bar Nuts.

1892 Eastland Ave., 615-262-8611
2312 12th Ave. S., 615-292-7794
www.jenis.com

# TRY A DIFFERENT KIND
## OF MEAT-AND-THREE
## AT SAVARINO'S CUCINA

If chicken and livers dressed with greens and mac & cheese isn't your cup of tea, you can have an entirely different kind of meat-and-three experience at Hillsboro Village's Savarino's. While it's hard to bypass the tantalizing sandwich options—named for notable Nashvillians—head upstairs to the cafeteria-style line, where Corrado Savarino himself just might be on hand to dish out homemade favorites like eggplant Parmesan, meatballs, lasagna, and a variety of made-from-scratch noodle dishes and salads. Save room for something sweet from the massive dessert spread.

2121 Belcourt Ave.
615-460-9878

FOODIE, KID FRIENDLY

# MUSIC & ENTERTAINMENT

# SEE A SHOW, ANY SHOW
## AT THE RYMAN AUDITORIUM

Birthed as the Union Gospel Tabernacle in the late 1800s, the "Mother Church" has been known as the Ryman Auditorium since 1904, when it hosted community events, operas, symphonies, political rallies, ballets, and theatrical productions. In 1943, the Ryman became the home of the Grand Ole Opry, bringing the brightest stars of country music to the radio airwaves. Though the Opry now resides out in Opryland, the Ryman's stage—which, along with the rest of the hall, has undergone extensive restoration—now hosts the brightest stars of every genre. Seeing a show there is a truly spiritual experience, and a must-do in Nashville.

116 5th Ave N.
615-889-3060
www.ryman.com

MUSIC, DATE NIGHT, HISTORIC

# Tip:

The Ryman is open daily from 9 to 4, offering self-guided tours of the historic structure, where you'll learn about the birth of bluegrass—which many believe took place on the Ryman stage in 1945—and the time that Houdini made an appearance (or a disappearance). A guided backstage tour lifts the curtain on one of the most famous, revered stages in the country, on which you can have your picture made during the tour.

# Did You Know?

The Fisk Jubilee Singers have been making history for more than a century, performing for kings and queens to raise money for their school in the late 19th century, and being invited by the U.S. Embassy to perform in Ghana in the early 21st century. In 2008, President George W. Bush awarded the Fisk Jubilee Singers a National Medal of Arts, the highest national honor for artists.

# GET A BEAUTIFUL
## MUSIC HISTORY LESSON
## FROM THE FISK JUBILEE SINGERS

In the late 1800s, the Fisk Jubilee Singers were the first group to publicly perform the songs of slaves, sharing the sacred spirituals with the rest of the world. They broke barriers then, entertaining European royalty, and today, the world-renowned a capella group continues to honor and preserve the legacy of this American musical tradition. Comprising vocally gifted Fisk University students, the group regularly tours the U.S. and abroad, but if you're lucky, you can catch them in one of their hometown performances for a truly emotional, stunning musical experience.

www.fiskjubileesingers.org

# CATCH A ROUND
## AT THE BLUEBIRD CAFE

Located in an unassuming strip mall in Green Hills, the Bluebird Cafe has earned a reputation as ground zero for the songwriting scene. The "in-the-round" style performances—songwriters sit together, often in a circle, and take turns playing their tunes, helping each other out—give fans an intimate listening experience in the 90-seat venue. If you want to hear the hit by the person who wrote it—and you never know, the star who sang it just might drop in, too—this is a must. Reservations are highly recommended, as the popularity and restrictive size of the venue usually leads to sellout crowds. We'd also recommend that you keep chatter to a minimum in this tiny room, unless you want to spend the night fending off dirty looks from strangers.

4104 Hillsboro Pk.
615-383-1461
www.bluebirdcafe.com

MUSIC, CLASSIC

# THINK YOU'VE GOT
## WHAT IT TAKES?

On Monday nights, the Bluebird has an Open Mic Night, where you can mingle with other songwriters, all of whom are eager to show of their new stuff and sharpen their skills. If you want to participate, the folks at the Bluebird recommend that you start lining up at, but not before, 4:30 on any given Monday. Open Mic sign-up is at 5:30, and you must be signed up by 5:45. Names are randomly drawn, and at 6:00, they announce the lineup, commencing the show. Each writer gets to play one or two original compositions to a the crowd. Since the focus is on the song, the writer cannot be accompanied by more than two other people, and drums and/or backing tracks are strictly prohibited.

Did You Know?
In the early '90s, the movie *The Thing Called Love*, which starred River Phoenix, Sandra Bullock, and Dermot Mulroney, also starred The Bluebird, making it a renowned venue past the city limits. *The Thing Called Love* was Phoenix's last film before his untimely death.

# ENJOY FREE MUSIC
## AT LIVE ON THE GREEN

This free, late-summer outdoor music series is presented by local independent radio station WRLT Lightning 100, bringing national acts and local favorites to thousands of music fans each week. Held in Public Square Park in downtown Nashville, the event is kid- and pet-friendly. Artists who have played this immensely popular event include Matt Nathanson, Michael Franti, Dr. John, the Wallflowers, Alabama Shakes, and Band of Horses. Get there early if you want to get a good spot, and spring for VIP tix if you want to sit in the fancy area with your own bar (and VIP porta-potties).

www.liveonthegreen.net

MUSIC, KID FRIENDLY, GREAT OUTDOORS

# HAVE A GRAND OLE TIME
## AT THE GRAND OLE OPRY

Catch the world's longest running live radio program show at the Opry Complex, where each performance features a who's who of country royalty, from legendary artists to rising stars. Many appearances are followed by autograph signings, and if you really want to get up close and personal, you can take a Grand Ole Opry tour—offered in the daytime, post-show, and at a VIP level that allows you to watch a song from the side of the stage—where you just might get to stand onstage yourself.

2804 Opryland Dr.
615-871-OPRY
www.opry.com

CLASSIC, MUSIC, HISTORIC

# AND WHILE YOU'RE AT OPRYLAND . . . GET ON A BOAT
## AT THE *GENERAL JACKSON SHOWBOAT*

Sure, it sounds corny, and it kind of is, but it's still fun. The General Jackson, docked in Opryland next to the enormous Opryland Hotel and the equally huge Opry Mills Mall, offers kid-friendly daytime and evening shows that take you on a trip down the Music Highway as you cruise down the Cumberland River. The daytime trip comes with a massive buffet (the evening option with a sit-down dinner), so you can really make a day—or a night—of it.

2812 Opryland Dr.
615-458-3900
www.generaljackson.com

KID FRIENDLY, THE GREAT OUTDOORS

# AND IF YOU'RE STILL AT OPRYLAND . . .
## VISIT THE GAYLORD OPRYLAND RESORT & CONVENTION CENTER AND OPRY MILLS

Even if you don't actually stay at the Opryland—the hotel is roughly 10 miles from downtown Nashville—you should at least stop in and take a look at this behemoth hotel. Skip the gym that day, because you'll get a workout walking from one end to the other, exploring the indoor atrium, a variety of specialty shops, and restaurants. If you have a golfer in the group, the 18-hole Gaylord Springs Golf Links is nearby, and shopaholics can enjoy over 200 stores just a short walk away at Opry Mills Mall.

2800 Opryland Dr.
866-972-6779
www.marriott.com/hotels

433 Opry Mills Dr.
615-514-1000
www.simon.com/mall/opry-mills

KID FRIENDLY, SHOPPING

# CATCH A MOVIE
## AT THE BELCOURT THEATRE

Nashville's arthouse theatre, The Belcourt, is an essential part of the community, bringing independent films to Nashville along with a variety of educational outreach and community engagement programs. Plus, the two-screen theatre has excellent popcorn, lots of local candy options, and a full bar, which makes all movies more enjoyable. On many weekends, they have midnight movies that skew toward the nostalgic (*Back to the Future*) and often, the ridiculous (*Xanadu*). The charming atmosphere of the beautiful old building, located in walkable Hillsboro Village, makes for a truly special cinematic experience.

2102 Belcourt Ave.
615-846-3150
www.belcourt.org

CULTURE, DATE NIGHT

# SING KARAOKE
## AT SANTA'S PUB

Right next to the state fairgrounds you'll find a double-wide, Santa-emblazoned trailer filled with everything from Nashville TV stars to sorority girls to *American Idol* stars to bikers (sometimes cyclists, sometimes motorcyclists). What could bring all of these seemingly disparate groups together? Well, Santa, of course . . . and karaoke. Run by Denzel "Santa" Irwin and his lovely wife Angelina, this cash-only, beer-only, smoker-friendly bar has the best karaoke and the best people-watching in Nashville.

2225 Bransford Ave.
615-593-1872
www.santaspub.com

ADULT BEVERAGES, MUSIC

# CELEBRATE THE LEGACY
## OF LIVE RADIO SHOWS
## AT MUSIC CITY ROOTS

Carrying on the tradition of old-time radio shows like the Grand Ole Opry's regular transmission on WSM (which broadcasts to this day), Music City Roots is a live musical variety show recorded at the barn at the Loveless Café. The two-hour show, which streams online and is broadcast on local radio station Hippie 94.5, celebrates Nashville's rich, diverse music scene, featuring a variety of artists that blur the lines among Americana, bluegrass, rockabilly, rock, world music, and folk. For a truly wonderful evening, grab an early dinner at Loveless Café before the show.

8400 Tennessee Hwy 100
615-646-9700
www.musiccityroots.com

MUSIC, SCENIC ROUTE

# SEE THE ROCKETTES
## (AND A LOT OF LIGHTS)
## AT THE OPRYLAND HOTEL

OK, we already told you about Opryland, but this one deserves its own page, because during the holidays, the Opryland Hotel turns into a winter wonderland, even if there's no frost on the ground outside. From mid-November on, you can see more than two million twinkling lights—take that, Clark Griswold!—and acres of impressive decorations including two million—yep, again—pounds of ice sculptures. Also, straight from Radio City Music Hall in NYC, we have over a month of special performances from The Rockettes at our Grand Ole Opry House. All of this is enough to melt any Grinch's heart.

2800 Opryland Dr.
615-889-1000
www.marriott.com

KID FRIENDLY, SCENIC, CLASSIC

# DANCE WITH A STRANGER
## AT ROBERT'S WESTERN WORLD

There are plenty of honky tonks to choose from on Lower Broad in downtown Nashville, but if you have to choose just one, we suggest giving your heart to Robert's. In addition to having some of the best classic country tunes in town—try to go on a night when house band Brazilbilly is playing; lead singer Jesse Lee Jones runs the joint—the tiny dance floor is as packed as the boot-lined walls, but with friendly strangers who would love to take you for a spin. And if you work up an appetite from all that dancing, you can grab The Recession Special—that's a fried bologna sandwich, a PBR, and a Moon Pie, all that and a bag of chips (no, really) for just $5.

416 Broadway
615-244-9552
www.robertswesternworld.com

MUSIC, CLASSIC, ADULT BEVERAGES
FOODIE, DATE NIGHT

# EXPERIENCE
## ONE OF THE BIGGEST MUSIC FESTS IN THE COUNTRY AT BONNAROO . . .

If you're looking to get out of the city for an extended weekend, why not go camping with 80,000 of your closest friends for Bonnaroo? Held on a 700-acre farm in Manchester—just an hour from Nashville—Bonnaroo's multiple stages and tents (good luck figuring out the difference between What Stage, Which Stage, This Tent, That Tent, and The Other Tent after a few beers in the blazing heat) feature the best in all genres of music, comedy, film, theater, and visual arts. But really, it's about the music; Paul McCartney played a killer set in 2013 that people are still talking about. If you're going to go, you really should resign yourself to multiple days of being sweaty and muddy (the fest is always in June), but the vibe is so good, you won't care.

800-594-8499
www.bonnaroo.com

MUSIC, GREAT OUTDOORS, SCENIC

# ... OR AT CMA
## MUSIC FESTIVAL

The CMA Music Fest—still affectionately known as "Fan Fair," which it was known as until 2004—is the largest gathering of country music fans in the country, and by far the largest festival in the city limits. In 2013, over 80,000 fans flocked to Nashville for four days of music, autograph signings, and sold-out nightly concerts at LP Field. Held for years at the Tennessee State Fairgrounds, the event is now centered in and around downtown, and Nashville residents know that the people-watching is as good as the music . . . and sometimes better. Like Bonnaroo, the fest is always in June, so bring lots of sunscreen and cool clothing.

www.cmaworld.com/cma-music-festival

MUSIC, GREAT OUTDOORS, SCENIC, KID FRIENDLY, CLASSIC

# BRING OUT YOUR INNER CHILD
## AT NASHVILLE CHILDREN'S THEATRE

As the nation's oldest professional theater for children, the Nashville Children's Theatre has been entertaining young theatergoers—and their parents—since 1931. Each season, NCT offers a diverse and exciting array of options, including musicals, comedies, and adaptations of classic children's books for kids of all ages. Check out any of the family-friendly shows at the theatre, located in downtown Nashville, and see why *Time* magazine ranked NCT as one of the top five children's theaters in the country.

25 Middleton St.
615-252-4675
www.nashvillechildrenstheatre.org

KID FRIENDLY, CULTURE

# HOWL AT THE MOON
## AT THE FULL MOON PICKIN' PARTY

This legendary bluegrass jam, held May through October at the Warner Park Stables, is held under the light of the full moon, and is one of the best bargains in town. The family-friendly, dog-friendly series gathers pickers of all levels, with headlining acts on a main stage and many auxiliary jams occurring around the grounds. The admission price ($15 in advance, $20 at the door) gets you water, soft drinks, and four beers, and you can purchase from a selection of food trucks on site. If you're a picker and you bring an "approved" instrument (check the website for a list), you get $5 off admission.

2500 Old Hickory Blvd.
615-370-8053
www.friendsofwarnerparks.com

KID FRIENDLY, GREAT OUTDOORS, MUSIC

# SEE A SHOW
## AT TPAC

In addition to bringing Nashville smash Broadway touring shows like *Jersey Boys*, *We Will Rock You,* and *Wicked*, the Tennessee Performing Arts Center (TPAC) showcases the best of local theater through regular performances by the Tennessee Repertory Theatre. TPAC, housed in the James K. Polk Cultural Center, also hosts performances by the Nashville Ballet and the Nashville Opera, and sits atop the Tennessee State Museum. Regardless of what kind of show you attend, be sure to stop at the Art-O-Mat in the lobby, where you can purchase handcrafted art for only $5 from a retrofitted cigarette machine.

505 Deaderick St.
615-782-4000
www.tpac.org

MUSIC, KID FRIENDLY, DATE NIGHT, CLASSIC, CULTURE

# CATCH SOME LIVE MUSIC
## AT THE CANNERY ROW COMPLEX

Located on 8th Avenue, close to downtown, the Gulch, midtown, and East Nashville, these three venues, located in the same building, have enough options to satisfy Goldilocks. With rooms in small (High Watt), medium (Mercy Lounge), and large (Cannery Ballroom), the complex offers concerts of all kinds, bringing a huge variety of bands and artists through the city, including Adele, Girl Talk, Spoon, St. Vincent, and Dawes. All of the venues have full bars and are non-smoking, although there are multiple patios for smokers. It's interesting to see a band grow their following from the smallest venue to the largest—or, as it sometimes goes in Music City, in the opposite direction.

1 Cannery Row
615-251-3020
www.mercylounge.com

MUSIC, ADULT BEVERAGES
DATE NIGHT, KID FRIENDLY

# SPORTS & RECREATION

# FIND OUT WHY WE'RE
## THE "ATHENS OF THE SOUTH"
## AT THE PARTHENON
## IN CENTENNIAL PARK

Perhaps you've been wondering why we have a full-scale replica of one of ancient Greece's most recognizable structures in Centennial Park. Located just across the way from Vanderbilt University, our Parthenon was originally built in 1897 for the Tennessee Centennial Exposition, exemplifying the city's motto, the "Athens of the South." This Parthenon, surrounded by trails, a sunken garden, and a lake, also boasts a massive 42-foot gold statue of Athena and an art gallery inside. Peruse the gallery walls and take a walk around the pretty park, or catch a performance by the Nashville Symphony or the Nashville Shakespeare Festival.

2500 West End Ave.
615-862-8431
www.nashville.gov/Parks-and-Recreation/Parthenon

GREAT OUTDOORS, KID FRIENDLY, HISTORIC

# SO WAIT,
## WHY ARE WE THE ATHENS OF THE SOUTH?

Long before anybody called Nashville "Music City," we were known as the "Athens of the South." This nickname, which originated in the second half of the 19th century, stemmed from Nashville's reputation as a city filled with education, art, architecture, and a sense of community in line with ancient Greek and Roman ideology.

The original Parthenon was not intended to be permanent, but was so popular with residents and visitors that when the original was demolished, a sturdier structure was erected in the 1920s. It remains a popular landmark today. In 1972, it was added to the National Register of Historic Places.

# GET IN TOUCH WITH NATURE
## AT CHEEKWOOD BOTANICAL GARDEN

Cheekwood, a 55-acre nature preserve built by the Cheek Family—of Maxwell House Coffee fame—features extensive gardens surrounding a stunning limestone mansion that serves as an art gallery and event space. In addition to a multitude of annual events that are usually family-friendly, Cheekwood hosts breathtaking outdoor installations—Chihuly and *LIGHT* by Bruce Munro were recent hits and indoor art exhibits, like 2013's envelope-pushing *More Love*. Cheekwood also serves as the host location for Nashville's most exclusive party, the Swan Ball.

1200 Forrest Park Dr.
615-356-8000
www.cheekwood.org

THE GREAT OUTDOORS, KID FRIENDLY

# WALK AND LEARN
## ON A WALKIN' NASHVILLE TOUR

What better way to really see a city than to take a walking tour? The Walkin' Nashville Music City Legends Tour, led by Grammy-nominated music journalist Bill DeMain, covers decades of musical history and is packed with fun trivia and insider anecdotes. Over two hours, you'll visit legendary downtown Nashville institutions like Printer's Alley, the Ryman Auditorium, Tootsie's Orchid Lounge, and Ernest Tubb Record Shop. The tour is suitable for adults and kids alike, and the affable DeMain has an encyclopedic knowledge of music history. Online reservations are encouraged.

615-499-5159
www.walkinnashville.com

KID FRIENDLY, MUSIC,
HISTORIC, THE GREAT OUTDOORS

# ENJOY AMERICA'S PASTIME
## AT A NASHVILLE SOUNDS GAME AT GREER STADIUM

We love our sports here in Nashville, including our minor league baseball team, the Nashville Sounds. The best night to go to Greer Stadium is on Throwback Thursdays, when you can get $2 draft beer and $2 snacks—we're talking about classic sporting event fare like hot dogs, popcorn, and nachos with bright orange cheese, which always tastes better at a baseball game. Sit close to the field or take in the game from Slugger's, located on the fourth floor of the stadium.

534 Chestnut St.
615-242-4371
www.nashvillesounds.com

DATE NIGHT, GREAT OUTDOORS, KID FRIENDLY, CLASSIC

● ● ● ● ● ● ● ● ● ● ● ● ● ● ● ● ● ● ● ● ● ● ●

# CHALLENGE YOURSELF
## AT ADVENTUREWORKS

Whether you're looking to bond with your coworkers or teach your kids about teamwork, a trip to Adventureworks will get the job done, and with guaranteed fun for all involved. Located in nearby Kingston Springs, Adventureworks offers a challenge course, ziplines, and aerial trekking, where you'll climb across a series of cables, logs, and ropes among the treetops. Adventureworks offers packages for groups and weekend outings, and even curates activities for fearless couples.

1300 Narrows Rd.
Kingston Springs
615-297-2250
www.adventureworks.com

GREAT OUTDOORS, KID FRIENDLY

## Tip:

Some of the activities at Adventureworks are more strenuous than others or have age restrictions, so make sure you alert the staff ahead of time so they know if you have any little ones in your party or adventurers with injuries.

# CLIMB THE STONE STEPS
## AT PERCY WARNER PARK

Located at the terminus of Nashville's ritziest road, Belle
Meade Boulevard, Percy Warner Park is part of Warner Parks,
2,684 acres of hiking trails, biking routes, an equestrian center,
and a golf course. The hiking trails range from rolling hills to
sharp ascents, but the steepest hill of all is at the origin of the
trail in the allee, the massive limestone steps that deposit you
at Warner Woods trailhead, a two-and-a-half mile loop. If you
can run all the way up those steps, well, you're in tip-top shape.
Fortunately, it's much easier on the way down ...

End of Belle Meade Blvd.
615-352-6299
www.nashville.gov/Parks-and-Recreation/Parks/Warner-Parks.aspx

GREAT OUTDOORS, SCENIC, KID FRIENDLY

# TAKE A SPIN AROUND THE CITY
## ON A NASHVILLE GREENBIKE OR A NASHVILLE B-CYCLE

Nashville is steadily growing more walkable and bikeable, and if you're looking to explore the city on two wheels but don't have your own bike, you can rent a GreenBike or a B-Cycle. The bright green GreenBikes are free, and the bright red B-Cycles have affordable memberships available in daily, weekly, monthly, or yearly options. Both can be checked out and in at various spots around the city; check the respective websites for rules and station locations.

www.nashvillegreenbikes.org
www.nashville.bcycle.com

GREAT OUTDOORS, SCENIC

# HAVE A NASHVILLE CONVERSATION
## ON THE PEDESTRIAN BRIDGE

Do you remember that episode of ABC's *Nashville* when Rayna and Deacon were having a deep conversation on the bridge? Well, you can take a walk on the Shelby Street Pedestrian Bridge, which connects East Nashville to West, offering easy access to events at LP Field. The bridge itself is a hot event spot, often rented out for weddings and other happenings in the city, from food and wine festivals to fitness events. The deep conversation is optional, but the stunning view of the famous Nashville skyline from the bridge begs for a photo op.

Located where Shelby Avenue meets the
Cumberland River in downtown Nashville.

DATE NIGHT, GREAT OUTDOORS, SCENIC ROUTE

## Tip:

*Nashville* superfans can visit the
many locations featured on the TV show,
like The 5 Spot, Cheekwood, and the
Schermerhorn Symphony Center. Our
thoughtful Convention and Visitors Bureau
has neatly catalogued them for you at
www.visitmusiccity.com.

# RUN, OR JUST WATCH,
## THE COUNTRY MUSIC MARATHON

The Country Music Marathon and Half Marathon is one of the biggest races in Competitor's Rock 'n' Roll Series, which holds events in major cities across the country. Held in late April each year, the course starts in front of Centennial Park, runs past the honky tonks of lower Broad and up Music Row, and snakes around the Belmont/12South neighborhood before heading through the Metro Center, downtown, and East Nashville, ending at L.P. Field. The race is as fun to watch as it is to run, with more than 30,000 people participating in the marathon and half-marathon, with 100,000 spectators cheering them on.

www.runrocknroll.competitor.com/nashville

GREAT OUTDOORS, SCENIC

# VISIT YOUR CHILDHOOD FRIENDS
## AT HILLWOOD STRIKE & SPARE

West Nashville's Hillwood Strike & Spare may look like a typical family entertainmentplex on the outside. But indoors—beyond the 42-lane bowling alley, the family fun center, the pizza parlor, the arcade, and the bar—you'll find a treasure nestled in the back, adjacent to the glow-in-the-dark miniature golf room: The Rock-afire Explosion. You know, the animatronic band from ShowBiz, in the '80s? Yes, this is one of only a couple of commercially functioning bands of Billy Bob, Mitzi Mozzarella, and Fatz the Gorilla (at press time, Looney Bird was broken) left in the entire country. If you ask the staff—most of whom were born in the '90s or later—they'll grudgingly turn "the creepy animals" on, and suddenly it's 1983 all over again.

3710 Annex Ave.
615-425-2695
www.strikeandsparebowling.com

KID FRIENDLY, ADULT BEVERAGES
OFFBEATENPATH, DATE NIGHT

# TEST YOUR BALANCE
## WITH PADDLEBOARD YOGA
## AT PADDLE UP TN

You may not think of watersports when you think of a land-locked state like Tennessee, but with the Cumberland River, Percy Priest, and Center Hill Lake easily accessible from the city, we have options. Paddleboarding is a fun, challenging workout on its own, but when you add yoga to the mix, be prepared to be humbled. This partnership of Hot Yoga Plus and Paddle Up TN at Rock Harbor Marine offers classes suitable for all levels. Because, no matter how "good" you are at yoga, you're going to fall in. The most fun you'll have working out, hands-down.

525 Basswood Ave.
615-496-8082
www.paddleuptn.com

GREAT OUTDOORS, SCENIC

# GET READY FOR SOME FOOTBALL
## AT LP FIELD

Nashville didn't have an NFL team to call its own until the late '90s, and any Titans or Oilers fan know it was a rocky road to get there. Perhaps that's why there's such a ferocious love for the team, in good seasons and in bad. Catching a home game at LP Field is a bucket list item for any Nashvillian, football fan or not. Your best bet is to park downtown and walk over one of the bridges to avoid that traffic jam that sequesters East Nashville during game time. Bonus? You get to enjoy a stunning view of the Nashville skyline when you walk back to your car.

1 Titans Way
615-565-4300
www.titansonline.com

GREAT OUTDOORS, KID FRIENDLY

# TAKE A TRIP
# DOWN THE RIVER
## AT TIP-A-CANOE

Since canoeing down the Cumberland River, which runs through downtown Nashville, would be kind of weird, we recommend trekking out to Kingston Springs. Located just 20 miles outside of the city, the lovely area is home to Tip-A-Canoe, where you can take the family for a canoe or kayak trip ranging from one to 10 hours. Those who want to earn their scouts' badges can partake in overnight trips, too, camping in the pretty countryside.

1279 Highway 70, Kingston Springs
800-550-5810
www.tip-a-canoe.com

GREAT OUTDOORS, KID FRIENDLY

# GO FAST
## AT THE FAIRGROUNDS SPEEDWAY

The second oldest continually operating track in the U.S. has seen many changes since the early 1900s, when people were amazed by cars that went faster than 60 mph. The Fairgrounds Speedway is now the home of the All-American 400, the renowned stock car race and the Speedway's biggest event of the season. Grandstand tickets are $10 and under (kids under five are free), and diehards can get a pit pass for $30.

625 Smith Ave.
615-254-1986
www.fairgroundsspeedwaynashville.com

KID FRIENDLY, GREAT OUTDOORS, CLASSIC

# HAVE A DAY AT THE RACES
## AT STEEPLECHASE

Our friends in Kentucky have their Derby, but we're particularly fond of our Iroquois Steeplechase. Commonly known as Steeplechase, this American Grade NSA-sanctioned horse race is held the second Saturday in May each year at beautiful Percy Warner Park. This daylong event, which is also a fundraiser for the Monroe Carell Jr. Children's Hospital at Vanderbilt, is filled with horse races—including stick-horse races for the kids— picnics, and a lot of adult beverages. Whether you're hanging out at one of the tailgating stations in the infield or at a boxholder's fancy mini-party in the ritzy, upper-deck area, a splendid time is guaranteed for all. Oh, and if it rained recently? Wear boots.

800-619-4802
For current entrance/parking information for Percy Warner Park
visit www.iroquoissteeplechase.org

GREAT OUTDOORS, KID FRIENDLY, ADULT BEVERAGES

# PICK A SIDE
## AT THE BATTLE OF THE BOULEVARD

Belmont University and Lipscomb University normally co-exist quite peacefully from their respective locations off Belmont Boulevard. Separated by just a couple of miles, the schools come together for the Battle of the Boulevard, when the Atlantic Sun Conference basketball teams face off. The Belmont Bruins first battled the Lipscomb Bisons in 1953, and they revisit this rivalry at least twice a year, much to the delight of the Nashville fans on either side of the court.

For game schedules, visit www.lipscombsports.com or
www.belmontbruins.com

KID FRIENDLY

# DO A FUN RUN
## WITH WHAT DO YOU RUN FOR?

Sports event management biz What Do You Run For? fuses running with philanthropy in the most fun way possible. While they work with many groups that bring competitive and fundraising runs to the Nashville area, their signature "I Run For The Party" series bridges the gap between exercising and partying. Whether you're doing a Cinco de Mayo or a St. Paddy's Day Kegs & Eggs Run, you'll race around the city with the promise of some sort of adult beverage at the end, or perhaps on the way. With 5K and 10K options in most races, they're open to all levels, even if you want to walk for the party.

www.whatdoyourunfor.com

# GET YOUR ENERGY OUT
## AT SKY HIGH SPORTS

What's great about indoor trampoline paradise Sky High Sports is that it's both the perfect rainy day antidote for restless kids and a fun way to trick adults into exercising. You can let your kids bounce with the masses, or book your own private "court" of trampoline floors and walls. While they kids are playing dodgeball, you can join an AIRobics class, where you'll burn over 1,000 calories in an hour workout. You'll be exhausted afterwards—and so will the kids—but it's seriously fun. Oh, and pro tip: Monitor how much of that snack bar pizza you the kids eat before they jump. Trust us.

5270 Harding Pl.
615-366-4252
www.jumpskyhigh.com

# CULTURE &
# HISTORY

# HAVE A FUN HISTORY LESSON
## AT THE COUNTRY MUSIC HALL OF FAME AND MUSEUM

The recently expanded museum is home to more than two million priceless items essential to country music history, from Kitty Wells's 1941 Martin guitar to Dolly Parton's handwritten lyrics to "Jolene." You'll spend hours perusing the video and audio clips and exhibits that serve as a crash course of the advent and evolution of country music. In addition to the permanent collection, rotating exhibits will entice fans of all ages.

222 5th Ave. S.
615-416-2001
www.countrymusichalloffame.org

HISTORIC, KID FRIENDLY, MUSIC

# ENJOY EVEN MORE
## COUNTRY MUSIC HALL OF FAME
## GOODNESS

The Country Music Hall of Fame and Museum preserves several of the city's creative and historic linchpins, including the historic RCA Studio B and Hatch Show Print. More than one thousand top-10 American hits were recorded at RCA Studio B, including over 150 recordings by Elvis Presley. You can sign up for a tour, which departs from the Country Music Hall of Fame and Museum, at www.countrymusichalloffame.org.

You'll also want to save time for a stop at Hatch Show Print, which moved from Lower Broad to 224 5th Ave. S. in late November 2013. Hatch Show is one of the oldest working letterpress print shops in the country—it started in 1879, creating posters for everything from turn-of-the-century vaudeville posters to whatever hot band is playing at the Ryman this weekend. They also do custom prints, like wedding invitations, so you can feel like a music legend even if you can't carry a tune. Learn more about Hatch Show at www.countrymusichalloffame.org.

HISTORIC, MUSIC

# GO PICKIN'
## AT ANTIQUE ARCHEOLOGY

It's not unusual to see a line of tourists—and, during the summer, lines of tour buses—swarming the front entrance of Antique Archeology, the retail outpost from Mike Wolfe, creator and star of the History Channel's "American Pickers." If geeking out over one-of-a-kind antiques isn't enough for you, the shop sells T-shirts, coffee mugs, and other Pickers swag. The store is located in Marathon Village, one of the city's most exciting commercial redevelopments, and if you get stuck in line for a bit, stop next door at Bang Candy Co. for their signature gourmet marshmallows, or—if the line is really long—a fresh panini.

1300 Clinton St. #130
615-810-9906
www.antiquearchaeology.com

HISTORIC, SHOPPING

# WHILE YOU'RE AT
## MARATHON VILLAGE...

Marathon Village is a block of buildings that formerly housed the Marathon Motor Works Factory, the earliest of which dates back to 1881. The Marathon motor car was manufactured here just after the turn of the 20th century, but the buildings were eventually neglected and shuttered until Barry Walker bought them in 1986, starting an extensive renovation project that continues to this day. You can learn more about this historic building and the Marathon motor car in the veritable museum that Walker has created in the office and administration building, just across the street from Antique Archeology. Today, the block-long building complex is home to some of the city's most exciting and gifted makers, like Emil Erwin, Otis James, and Bang Candy Co.

1305 Clinton St.
615-327-1010
www.marathonvillage.com

HISTORIC

## Tip:

Hit the Frist during one of their popular Frist Fridays events, which occurs the last Friday of each month throughout the summer. In addition to gaining access to the galleries, attendees enjoy food and drinks on the beautiful back patio and lawn of the Frist while being entertained by live music, often thematically tied to the exhibits inside. For example, 2013's *Sensuous Steel: Art Deco Automobiles* show was nicely accented by a performance by Drivin' N' Cryin'. Pun intended, and thoroughly enjoyed.

Admission is free for members and only $10 for everyone else.

# ENJOY A DAY OF ART
## AT THE FRIST CENTER
## FOR THE VISUAL ARTS

Our local visual arts center is housed in a stunning Art Deco building that formerly served as Nashville's main post office. Since 2001, the walls of the Frist have welcomed some of the most exciting art shows to tour the country, from the acclaimed *Warhol Live* to the Victoria & Albert Museum's exciting *Golden Age of Couture* fashion extravaganza. The Martin ArtQuest Gallery offers interactive, inventive fun for kids of all ages with 30 stations that encourage learning and creative thinking.

919 Broadway
615-244-3340

www.fristcenter.org

KID FRIENDLY, DATE NIGHT

# GO TO THE SOURCE
## AT UNITED RECORD PRESSING

Now that you've bought some vinyl, go see how it's made at United Record Pressing, the site where the first Beatles' 7-inch discs were pressed in America for Vee Jay Records in 1962. On the tour, which is given only at 11 A.M. on Fridays, you'll learn how vinyl is made in the factory, which is quite busy these days with the resurging interest in vinyl. You'll also get to see the Motown Suite, an apartment above the factory that accommodated guests and clients from Vee Jay and Motown in the '60s, and the party room, which was used as an event space for label signing parties.

453 Chestnut St.
615-259-9396
www.urpressing.com

MUSIC, HISTORIC

# TRAVEL THE WORLD WITHOUT LEAVING THE CITY LIMITS
## AT THE GLOBAL EDUCATION CENTER

The Global Education Center, located in West Nashville near Sylvan Park, is a nonprofit that promotes global awareness and helps find a common thread between all cultures through arts education. The center offers a variety of after-school programs and classes, community concerts, arts camps, workshops, and events for all ages. Check the website for a current schedule and pricing at what might be the only place in Nashville where you can take djembe, belly dance aerobics, and Chinese dance for children classes, all in the same week.

4820 Charlotte Ave.
615-292-3023
www.globaleducationcenter.net

KID FRIENDLY, CULTURE, SHOPPING

# TURN THE PAGE
## AT THE SOUTHERN FESTIVAL OF BOOKS

For more than two decades, Humanities Tennessee has turned Nashville into the southern capital of books throughout the second weekend of October. This free event celebrates the joy of reading, attracting renowned authors from around the country and giving readers and writers a chance to interact. With author reading sessions, panel discussions, book signings, and a variety of programs and literary performances, there's something for all ages and for every bookworm.

Held annually on the second weekend in October;
schedule and more information at www.humanitiestennessee.org

KID FRIENDLY

# VISIT THE AREA'S OLDEST GHOSTS
## AT THE NASHVILLE CITY CEMETERY

OK, cemeteries aren't for everybody, but those who aren't easily creeped out will appreciate a slightly morbid history lesson. The oldest public cemetery in Nashville dates back to 1822 and is open from dawn until dusk, serving as a final resting place for some of the area's most prominent individuals. Among the 23,000-plus dearly departed are city founders, Confederate generals, roughly two dozen Nashville mayors, and former slaves. The cemetery, after falling victim to neglect and vandalism for decades, underwent significant restoration by the Metro Historical Commission. Scheduled tours are available—sign up in advance at their website—or feel free to walk around at your own pace.

1001 4th Ave. S.
www.thenashvillecitycemetery.org

HISTORIC, GREAT OUTDOORS

# SEE ANOTHER REASON WHY WE'RE THE ATHENS OF THE SOUTH
## AT THE NASHVILLE PUBLIC LIBRARY'S DOWNTOWN BRANCH

Hemingway once said "There is no friend as loyal as a book."
And if you're just borrowing your "friends" from a library,
you should really go to the downtown branch. The massive
300,000-square-foot modern classical building houses many
literary treasures and boasts a nonfiction section that spans the
length of a football field. The building is filled with beautiful
art; the Grand Reading Room features an installation titled "The
Story of Nashville," told through 80 hammered copper repoussé
panels. Even if you don't have a library card—shame on you!—
the building is a lovely place to wander around.

615 Church St.
615-862-5800
www.library.nashville.org

CLASSIC

# CATCH A FREE RIDE
## ON THE MUSIC CITY CIRCUIT

OK, we're the first to admit that public transportation has a long way to go in Nashville, but the Metro Transit Authority's Music City Circuit shows promise. These free buses, coded as Green, Blue, or Purple, connect downtown destinations like Bridgestone Arena, Schermerhorn Symphony Center, Ryman Auditorium, TPAC, and the Country Music Hall of Fame. The Green Circuit's stops are walkable to most of the touristy sites and runs until 11 P.M., so that's usually your best bet. Check the Metro Transit Authority's website for an updated schedule, or just keep your eye out for that friendly green bus.

www.nashvillemta.org

KID FRIENDLY, SCENIC ROUTE

# EXPLORE MODERN ART HISTORY
## AT THE FIRST SATURDAY ART CRAWL

On the first Saturday of each month, from 6 to 9 P.M., more than 20 of the art galleries of downtown Nashville host a fabulous free art crawl, welcoming art enthusiasts in for an unparalleled, eclectic mix of exhibits. Centered in the visual art hub of the city—downtown's Fifth Avenue, known as the Avenue of the Arts, and the upstairs of the Arcade—many of the stops offer free food and wine. And should you feel inclined to purchase some original art from local artists or visiting exhibitors, you'll certainly have the opportunity to comparison shop.

www.nashvilledowntown.com/play/first-saturday-art-crawl

DATE NIGHT, ADULT BEVERAGES, SHOPPING

# REVISIT THE BARD
## AT THE NASHVILLE SHAKESPEARE FESTIVAL

The Nashville Shakespeare Festival is both an educational outreach program and a troupe that provides free, professional outdoor performances of Shakespeare. Since their inception in 1988, more than a quarter of a million people have attended their lauded performances. While they are active year-round, their Shakespeare in the Park series, held annually in Centennial Park at the end of the summer, is a wonderful family excursion or date night.

www.nashvilleshakes.org

GREAT OUTDOORS, KID FRIENDLY, DATE NIGHT

# VISIT THE STARS
## AT THE MUSIC CITY WALK OF FAME

In a particularly musical area of Music City lies Walk of Fame Park, sandwiched between the Country Music Hall of Fame, the Schermerhorn Symphony Center, and the Bridgestone Arena, home to some of the biggest live shows in town. The Music City Walk of Fame honors legends of our local music, songwriting, and music industry community for the significant contributions they've made in preserving our unique musical heritage in Nashville and beyond. The pretty park is a nice place to have a brown-bag lunch, or get a photo op with the pavement stars, honoring everyone from Emmylou Harris to Kings of Leon.

On Demonbreun St. between 4th and 6th
www.visitmusiccity.com/walkoffame

GREAT OUTDOORS, KID FRIENDLY, CLASSIC

# SEE WHO
# WROTE THE HITS
## AT THE NASHVILLE SONGWRITERS
## HALL OF FAME

In Nashville, we honor the songwriters the same way that we honor the stars who sang the songs. Located in the shiny new Music City Center just across the street from the Country Music Hall of Fame, the Nashville Songwriters Hall of Fame Gallery pays homage to nearly 200 Hall of Fame members through an interactive exhibit. Patrons can learn about the writers behind some of the biggest hits of every genre of music through giant touchscreens, providing a quick master class about the masters of songcraft.

Music City Center entrance at corner of Demonbreun and 6th Ave.
www.nashvillesongwritersfoundation.com/hall-of-fame

MUSIC, KID FRIENDLY, CLASSIC

# HAVE A HISTORY LESSON WITHOUT CRACKING A BOOK
## AT THE HERMITAGE

If you're looking to brush up on your knowledge of the seventh U.S. president, visit President Andrew Jackson's former abode. After a short video providing some background on Mr. Jackson, you're led through a tour with informed guides dressed in period garb. Jackson's mansion sits on 1,120 acres with many historic buildings, archeological sites, and gardens—one of which houses the graves of Jackson and his wife Rachel—where you can freely wander after you tour the mansion. Wear comfortable shoes, as there's lots of walking on this one.

4580 Rachels Ln.
615-889-2941
www.thehermitage.com

HISTORIC, KID FRIENDLY

# HAVE ANOTHER HISTORY LESSON WITHOUT CRACKING A BOOK
## ON THE BATTLE OF NASHVILLE TOUR

If you really want to knock out a bunch of Nashville history at once, you can take the Battle of Nashville Tour. For only $30, you'll tour three historic homes: the Belle Meade Mansion, the Belmont Mansion, and the Travellers Rest Plantation & Museum. All three properties are must-see items on any Civil War buff's checklist, and we suggest hitting the Belle Meade Mansion last, because they have a winery.

www.tennesseecivilwar.com

HISTORIC, KID FRIENDLY

# SHOPPING & FASHION

# MAKE A RECORD
## AT THIRD MAN RECORDS

You know those awful, karaokesque booths—usually located in a mall or an amusement park—where you could record your own hit song? Yeah, this is nothing like that. Housed in the headquarters of Jack White's Third Man Records, the Third Man Recording Booth offers a unique recording experience. The Voice-o-Graph machine from 1947 can record up to two minutes of audio, creating a 6-inch vinyl record. A few instruments are available if you need one, and those who aren't musically inclined could read a poem, or record a message … and perhaps send it to a long-lost lover. A truly unique experience brought to you by one of Nashville's most beloved adopted sons, Jack White.

623 7th Ave. S.
615-891-4393
www.thirdmanrecords.com

MUSIC, KID FRIENDLY

# SEARCH FOR TREASURES
## AT GAS LAMP ANTIQUES
## AND DECORATING MALL

Even if you're not quite sure what you're looking for, GasLamp Antiques is the place to find it. Whether you visit the original building, or the extension just down the street at 128 Powell Place, there is truly something for everyone. GasLamp boasts more than 50,000 square feet packed with more than 300 dealers offering everything from furniture to jewelry to art to clothing to one-of-a-kind knickknacks for your home. Even if you just want to look around, the buildings are spacious, with plenty of room between each vendor area, and it's conveniently located just off I-65.

100 Powell Pl.
615-297-2224
www.gaslampantiques.com

SHOPPING, KID FRIENDLY

# BUY SOME MUSIC IN MUSIC CITY
## AT GRIMEY'S NEW & PRELOVED MUSIC

You really can't leave Music City without buying some music. In addition to a great selection of new and used CDs, vinyl, and DVDs, Grimey's has the latest from the big names to local bands, and lots of classic, rare, hard-to-find stuff, too. The staff is happy to help without any of that cliché music-nerd attitude, or you can peruse the staff picks or current charts for something new. Follow them on Twitter to stay in the know about in-store events; their free in-store performances have packed the house for the likes of BRMC, Paramore, Against Me!, and Nashville transplants The Black Keys.

1604 8th Ave. S.
615-254-4801
www.grimeys.com

MUSIC, SHOPPING

# WHILE YOU'RE THERE...
# STOP NEXT DOOR
# OR DOWNSTAIRS
## AT GRIMEY'S TOO AND THE BASEMENT

When you're done at Grimey's, pop next door to Grimey's Too, home to independent bookstore Howlin' Books and Frothy Monkey coffee bar. Also, Grimey's sits above one of the city's best venues, The Basement, a tiny room that provides an intimate environment for up-and-coming bands, industry showcases, and big acts alike (Metallica played a famous secret show here a few years ago). There's a full bar and a covered, heated patio for smokers, and there's early and late show offerings many nights of the week. Check out New Faces Nite, a free show of short sets from next-big-things that happens every Tuesday.

1702 8th Ave. S.
615-942-9683
www.howlinbooks.com

1604 8th Ave. S. #330
615-254-8006
www.thebasementnashville.com

MUSIC, SHOPPING, ADULT BEVERAGES

⬤ ⬤ ⬤ ⬤ ⬤ ⬤ ⬤ ⬤ ⬤ ⬤ ⬤ ⬤ ⬤ ⬤ ⬤ ⬤ ⬤ ⬤ ⬤ ⬤

# CHECK OUT THE BEST FLOOR IN NASHVILLE
## AT OLDMADEGOOD

East Nashville's Oldmadegood is run by two badass ladies who have an affinity for the unique and the lovingly repurposed. After outgrowing their previous Riverside Village outpost, they moved up Gallatin Road to bigger digs for their haul of vintage clothing, one-of-a-kind home goods, art, handmade jewelry, and creatively refurbished furniture. Oh, and they also have a ridiculously sparkly gold glitter floor that is hands-down the coolest floor in Nashville, and maybe the whole world. Seriously, it's mesmerizing.

3701B Gallatin Pk.
615-432-2882
www.oldmadegood.com

SHOPPING, OFF THE BEATEN PATH

# BUY THE PERFECT JEANS
## AT IMOGENE + WILLIE

For anyone who still thinks that "Nashville fashion" means rhinestones and cowboy boots, a stop in Imogene + Willie will erase that misperception. Located in booming 12South in an old gas station, the revered denim purveyors—run by husband-and-wife duo Matt and Carrie Eddmenson—offer timeless, well-constructed men's and women's clothing and home goods, but they're known far and wide for their jeans. The helpful staff will assist you with finding the perfect fit, and they offer gratis alterations with purchase, ensuring that you'll love these jeans forever and ever.

2601 12th Ave. S.
615-292-5005
www.imogeneandwillie.com

SHOPPING

# BUY A PAIR OF FOREVER SHOES
## AT PETER NAPPI

We may live in a buy-one-get-one-free, instant-gratification world, but thankfully, there are still artisans creating handmade, quality goods that you'll have forever. Peter Nappi clearly falls in the latter category with their superior, handcrafted men's and women's shoes and bags, displayed in one of the most breathtaking showrooms in the city. You won't find cowboy boots here, but timeless, Italian-crafted designs from this family-run business. If you can't spring for the shoes, check out the superior, unique jewelry and vintage clothing and home goods options.

1308 Adams St.
615-248-3310
www.peternappi.com

SHOPPING

# ... BUT IF YOU WANT COWBOY BOOTS,
## BUY SOME AT BOOT COUNTRY

As you're walking around Lower Broad in downtown Nashville, you're going to see a lot of boot stores among the honky tonks and kitschy gift shops. But you really can't beat **Boot Country**, home of the legendary buy-one-get-two-free boot deal. The boots aren't cheap, but when you split the price three ways, you're getting a great deal. Take a couple of friends or get boots for the whole family and you'll come out on top.

304 Broadway
615-259-1691

SHOPPING

# BRING OUT YOUR INNER PINUP, OR PERHAPS JUST YOUR INNER COWGIRL
## AT KATY K'S

Established in NYC in the early '80s, Katy K has been one of the sparkly stars in the Nashville fashion scene since the mid-'90s. Her 12th Avenue South outpost has new and vintage men's, women's, and children's clothing, but the focus is on retro styles from pin-up worthy dresses to Rockabilly Western shirts. Tucked in the front corner is Closet Case Vintage, a nicely curated mix of vintage clothing from the 1920s to the 1980s and authentic Edwardian- and Victorian-era pieces.

2407 12th Ave. S.
615-297-4242
www.katyk.com

SHOPPING, CLASSIC, KID FRIENDLY

# DIG FOR GOLD
## AT THE NASHVILLE FLEA MARKET

On the fourth weekend of every month, the Tennessee State Fairgrounds transforms the Expo Center into a massive flea market featuring vendors from over 30 states. If you're in the mood to buy some furniture, antiques, jewelry, clothing, or other doodads, there's a huge selection ranging from bargain to artisan. Pros, you probably already know, but day two is better for bargaining. It's $5 to park on site; otherwise admission is free.

625 Smith Ave.
615-862-8980
www.nashvilleexpocenter.org

SHOPPING, KID FRIENDLY, CLASSIC

# SHOP LOCAL
## AT THE IDEA HATCHERY

Located on the edge of East Nashville's busy Five Points Neighborhood, an eclectic epicenter of restaurants, bars, shops, and other businesses make up The Idea Hatchery – Five Points Collaborative. Conceived as a small business incubator, the Hatchery consists of eight small buildings—none larger than 320 square feet—which serve as a launch pad for young businesses in a collaborative environment that fosters community and growth. Browse the vintage clothing and impressive cowboy-boot wall at Goodbuy Girls, the fun, unique gifts at Alegria, or hyperlocal bookstore East Side Story. Whatever you end up buying, you'll eventually be able to say that you knew them when . . .

1108 Woodland St.
www.theideahatchery.net

SHOPPING, KID FRIENDLY

# PACK A PICNIC AND RUN TO THE HILLS
## AT ARRINGTON VINEYARD

Located on 75 acres of beautiful rolling hills in Williamson County just 25 miles south of Nashville is Arrington Vineyards. Owned by Brooks & Dunn's Kix Brooks, the young vineyard offers free tastings and sells gourmet chocolates, cheese, meats, and crackers. For a lovely day trip escape, pack a picnic basket and purchase wine by the bottle from their homey tasting room. The vineyard offers live music—see the website for the schedule—and plenty of indoor and outdoor seating to accommodate large groups.

6211 Patton Rd., Arrington
615-395-0102
www.arringtonvineyards.com

SCENIC, DATE NIGHT, GREAT OUTDOORS

# VISIT SOME FINE-STRINGED FRIENDS
## AT GRUHN GUITARS

In 2013, Gruhn Guitar moved from Lower Broadway to 8th Avenue, where George Gruhn and Co. have plenty of room for the 1,100-plus stringed instruments they stock. Gruhn and his knowledgeable staff will help you pick the perfect axe from their massive inventory of new guitars—including brands like Martin, Taylor, Collings, McPherson, and National Resophonic, to name a few—and vintage gems. Whether you're looking for an electric or acoustic, a mandolin or a banjo, a ukulele or a steel, chances are it's here. And if you just want to drool over the pretty instruments, that's OK too; just ask a staffer for assistance before you touch them.

2120 8th Ave. S.
615-256-2033
www.gruhn.com

MUSIC, SHOPPING, CLASSIC

# SHOP LIKE AN '80S ICON
## AT TIFFANY'S BOUTIQUE

After singing in malls across America in the '80s, it's only natural that pop icon Tiffany would have a boutique. She has two, in fact—one in nearby White House, and one in East Nashville. Both locations of Tiffany's Boutique offer vintage clothing, custom designed tie-dye dresses, and accessories and designs that Tiffany wore on red carpets. Who knows, if you're lucky, you might run into Tiffany herself at one of the stores! Jean jacket optional (but recommended).

301 Hwy. 76
White House, 615-672-3868

1006 Fatherland, Suite 201
615-559-5248
www.tiffanysboutique.com

SHOPPING, OFF THE BEATEN PATH, MUSIC

# SHOP LIKE A LEGEND
## AT MANUEL EXCLUSIVE CLOTHIER

The name "Manuel" is synonymous with classic Nashville fashion, as proprietor Manuel Cuevas' original designs have adorned presidents, athletes, movie stars, and a pantheon of music legends including Johnny Cash, Elvis, Bob Dylan, and, more recently, Jack White. Visit the Rhinestone Rembrandt's shop, where all of the men's and women's clothing is made in house and by hand, and try some of these expertly crafted garments on for size. You can go all-out, investing in a show-stopping jacket, or maybe dip a toe in with a rhinestone-encrusted belt.

800 Broadway
615-321-5444
www.manuelcouture.com

SHOPPING, CLASSIC

# SUPPORT THE MAKERS
## AT THE TACA CRAFT FAIRS

The Tennessee Association of Craft Artists (TACA) is a nonprofit that supports and promotes artists of all genres, and their massive craft fairs—held in both the spring and the fall—attract thousands each year. The juried event features more than 200 artists offering handcrafted jewelry, furniture, home goods, art, clothing, and more. TACA requires that the artist be onsite for the event, so you can meet the maker and get the story behind your newfound treasure. Held in beautiful Centennial Park, the free event includes lots of food trucks and live music and is family-friendly.

2500 West End Ave.
615-736-7600
www.tacacraftfair.com

GREAT OUTDOORS, KID FRIENDLY, SHOPPING

## Tip:

The Winery at the Belle Meade Plantation is one of the few places—outside of restaurants and bars—where you can legally purchase bottled wine on a Sunday. (Arrington Vineyards is another option.) In Nashville, liquor stores are closed on Sundays, and the sale of wine and liquor is not permitted in grocery stores. So, plan ahead if getting tipsy is on your itinerary.

# TAKE A WALK DOWN
## MAIN STREET IN FRANKLIN

Franklin, roughly a 25-minute drive from downtown Nashville, has the most charming main drag in their historic downtown area. For a perfect day trip, grab breakfast at Franklin Mercantile and wander around the cute antique shops a few blocks away from Main Street—Scarlett Scales always has fun findings—to work up an appetite for lunch. Hit Puckett's for an XL meat-and-three plate before you hit the shops on Main, which range from upscale boutiques like Haven, to the incredible new and used bookstore Landmark Booksellers, to sweet gift shops like Lulu. Hit McCreary's for some authentic Irish grub and brews. Although you'll be stuffed, pick up some cupcakes from IveyCake for the ride home.

Franklin Mercantile, 100 4th Ave. N., Franklin, 615-790-9730
www.franklinmercantile.com
Scarlett Scales, 246 2nd Ave. S., Franklin, 615-791-4097
www.scarlettscales.com
Puckett's, 120 4th Ave. S., Franklin, 615-794-5527
www.puckettsgrocery.com
Haven, 343 Main St., Franklin, 615-790-7954, www.sanctuaryofstyle.com
Landmark Booksellers, 114 E. Main St., Franklin, 615-791-6400
www.landmarkbooksellers.com
Lulu, 345 Main St., Franklin, 615-794-3345, www.lulufranklin.com
McCreary's Irish Pub, 414 Main St., Franklin, 615-591-3197
www.mccrearyspub.com

GREAT OUTDOORS, SHOPPING, KID FRIENDLY, FOODIE

• • • • • • • • • • • • • • • • • • • • • • • • •

# TAKE THE SPIRIT OF NASHVILLE HOME
## AT ANDERSON DESIGN GROUP

Local graphic design firm Anderson Design Group has been making iconic images of the most beloved landmarks in our beautiful city through their "Spirit of Nashville" series since 1993. Their studio store, which reopened in late 2013, offers a variety of their popular posters, T-shirts, calendars, postcards, and gifts featuring the Nashville series alongside many other collections (the retro-inspired Art and Soul of America series is a favorite). If you stop in the store, be sure to check out their Maker's Market, where you can assemble the perfect gift basket sourced from a curated group of area artisans.

116 29th Ave. N.
615-327-9894
www.andersondesigngroupstore.com

SHOPPING, CLASSIC

# SUGGESTED ITINERARIES

## CLASSIC

# FOODIE

# MUSIC

# DATE NIGHT

• • • • • • • • • • • • • • • • • • • • • • • • •

## ADULT BEVERAGES

# GREAT OUTDOORS

# KID FRIENDLY

• • • • • • • • • • • • • • • • • • • • • • • • •

## HISTORIC

## SHOPPING

## SCENIC ROUTE

# ACTIVITIES
## BY SEASON

You'll either love or hate Nashville weather—sure, the summers can be brutal, but we have long, lovely spring and fall, and only get the occasional freeze during winter. If visiting, you may want to plan ahead according to season, because, the rumors are true—if there's a chance of snow, things close, so call ahead. That being said, here are the ideal times to try the following:

### WINTER

Adventure Science Center, 72
Jack Daniel's Distillery, 37
Music City Roots, 55
Oak Bar, 28, 29
Ryman Auditorium, 42, 70, 101
RCA Studio B, 91
Prince's Hot Chicken, 4
Santa's Pub, 54

### SPRING

Battle of Nashville Tour, 107
Centennial Park, 66, 78, 103, 129
Country Music Marathon, 78
General Jackson Showboat, 50
Nashville City Cemetery, 99

## SUMMER

## FALL

• • • • • • • • • • • • • • • • • • • • • • • • •

# INDEX

• • • • • • • • • • • • • • • • • • • • • • • • •

• • • • • • • • • • • • • • • • • • • • • • •